SCIENCE THROUGH

Air

Hilary Devonshire

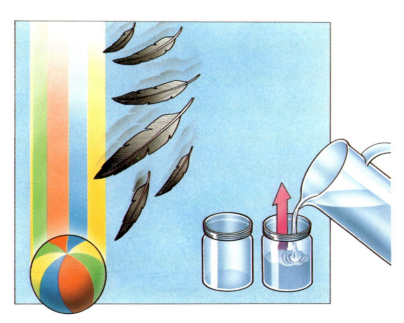

W
FRANKLIN WATTS
NEW YORK • LONDON • SYDNEY

© 1991 Franklin Watts

Paperback edition 1997

First published in Great Britain in 1991 by
Franklin Watts
96 Leonard Street
London EC2A 4RH

First America edition by
Franklin Watts
A Division of Grolier Publishing Co., Inc.
Sherman Turnpike
Danbury, Connecticut 06813

Franklin Watts Australia
14 Mars Road
Lane Cover
NSW 2066

ISBN 0 7496 0676 2 (hardback)
ISBN 0 7496 2739 5 (paperback)

10 9 8 7 6 5 4 3 2 1

Series editor: Hazel Poole
Edited by: Cleeve Publishing Services Limited
Designer: K & Co
Photographer: Chris Fairclough
Consultant: Henry Pluckrose, Margaret Whalley

A CIP catalogue record for this book is available from the British Library

Typeset by Lineage, Watford

Printed in Great Britain

CONTENTS

Equipment and materials *4*
Introduction *5*
Air is all around *6*
Air has weight *10*
Air pressure *12*
Moving air *13*
Wind strength *17*
Wind direction *19*
Wind can turn *21*
Wind can push *25*
Air supports *28*
Further ideas *30*
Glossary *31*
Index *32*

EQUIPMENT AND MATERIALS

This book describes activities which use the following:

Adhesives (PVA, cold water paste; UHU)
Adhesive tape – single-sided tape
               – double-sided tape
Balloons
Balsa wood
Beads
Bin liner
Bottle-tops (plastic)
Bowl
Bulldog clips
Card – strong
     – thin
Compass
Pair of compasses
Cork
Craft knife
Dish (shallow)
Dowel rod
Drinking straws (plastic)
Felt-tip pens
Food colouring
Glass jars (small)
Glycerine (obtainable at the local chemist shop)
Hairdryer
Inks – Indian
     – marbling
Knitting needle (metal)
Margarine carton
Night-light candle
Paintbrush
Paints – acrylic paints
       – water-colour paints
Paper – coloured paper
      – sugar paper
      – tissue paper (coloured)
      – tissues
      – white paper
Paper clips
Pen (black)
Pencil
Pins (headed)
Pipe-cleaners
Plant supports
Plate (small)
Rulers – plastic ruler
       – metal ruler, for use with the craft knife
Sand
Scissors
Sequins
Sponge
String
Sticks (wooden meat skewers)
Stop-clock
Thread
Tray (small)
Washing-up liquid
Washing-up liquid bottle
Water
Wire (thin, for example, florist's wire)
Wood
Yoghurt pots

INTRODUCTION

Air is all around us. It is indoors and outside. We breathe it, but cannot see it, smell it or taste it. It forms the atmosphere in which we live and is held around the surface of the Earth by the Earth's gravity.

Air is an invisible mixture of gases, mainly nitrogen and oxygen. The oxygen, which we breathe, is made by the plants of the Earth. If there were no plants, there would be no oxygen, and without oxygen we could not live.

By following the investigations in this book you will learn something about the science of air. At the start of each section there are some scientific ideas to be explored. A scientist looks at ideas and tries to discover if they are always true, and will also investigate to see if they can be *disproved*. You will be working like a scientist. A scientist is curious and wants to find out about the world in which we live. A scientist tests ideas, makes investigations and experiments, and tries to explain what has happened. Your results may be surprising or unexpected, and then you will find that you need to carry out a new investigation, or test a new idea.

You will also be an artist. You will be using air in the art activities in each section. For some of the activities you will be drawing designs for working models. A picture of an idea is useful to help you see how different parts might fit together and what shapes might be used. Through working with both air and the various art materials and techniques, you will make discoveries about how air behaves, and how air can be used. Your finished art work, designs and models will be a record of your scientific findings.

AIR IS ALL AROUND

Air is all around us but we cannot see it, smell it or taste it. It is an invisible mixture of gases. A gas will fill all the space inside any container.

Air spreads to fill the whole jar.

Liquid forces the air out to fill the jar.

Go outside on a calm, still day. Look at the air. If it is clear, the air is fresh and clean. Often the air in large towns and cities becomes polluted by industry and traffic exhaust fumes, and it becomes less clear and might even smell.
Have you smelt polluted air?

Seeing air

You will need: a bowl of water, a small glass jar, some food colouring and a paper tissue.

1. Put a little food colouring in the water. Push the paper tissue into the bottom of the small jar. Hold the jar vertically over the water.

2. Lower the jar gently, straight down, until it is right under the surface.

3. Lift the jar again. The tissue is still dry. The air in the jar has kept the water out. Did you see the air? What happens if you lower the jar into the water at an angle?

Blowing air

You will need: a bowl of water, a small glass jar, some food colouring and a flexible straw.

1. Fill a jar with coloured water.

2. Hold it up out of the water vertically, keeping the rim of the jar under water. The air pressing down on the surface of the water in the bowl will stop the water in the jar from running out.

3. Using a flexible straw, bend the end up under the rim of the jar and blow gently. Watch the jar slowly fill with air.

Bubble art

You will need: a jar, pre-mixed water-colour paint, washing-up liquid, a straw, and some white paper.

1. Squeeze a little washing-up liquid into the jar and add an equal quantity of paint. Use the straw to blow into the mixture. Watch the air bubbles rise over the rim of the jar. The air has been trapped by the soapy solution, which forms an elastic skin around the air.

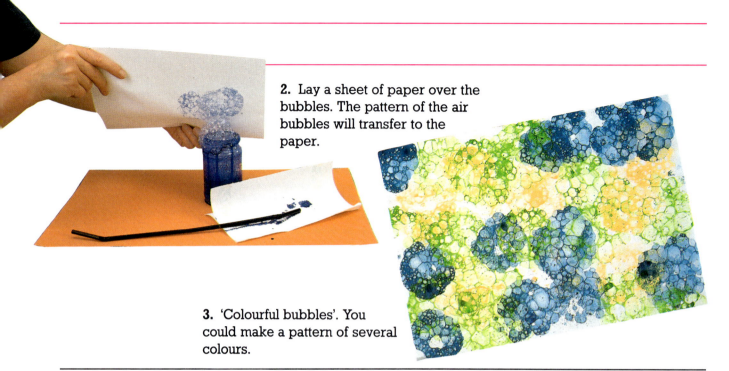

2. Lay a sheet of paper over the bubbles. The pattern of the air bubbles will transfer to the paper.

3. 'Colourful bubbles'. You could make a pattern of several colours.

Bubble dome

You will need: a shallow dish, pre-mixed water-colour paint, washing-up liquid, a straw, and some white paper.

2. Choose one bubble at the side. Put your straw inside it and blow gently and evenly to get a large bubble. You can then see right inside your dome!

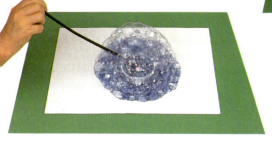

3. When you have finished watching your dome, allow the bubbles to die away. They will leave a bubble pattern around your dish.

1. Place the shallow dish on a piece of paper and fill it with your soap and paint mixture. Blow bubbles as before, but this time let the bubbles flow over the edge of the dish onto the paper. Blow a large dome of bubbles. Study your air bubbles. Are they all the same size? What shape are they? What happens to neighbouring bubbles when one bursts? Pop one and see. Is the soap skin moving around the air in the bubbles?

4. 'Bubble ring' left by the bubble dome.

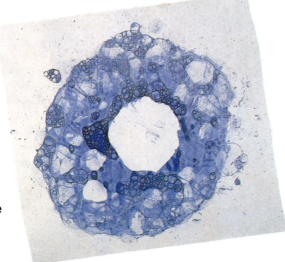

Are all bubbles round?

You will need: thin wire, a bowl of soapy water.

Make some different shaped bubble flowers with thin wire. Can you blow a triangular bubble?

A giant bubble

You will need: one metre of string, two plastic drinking straws, some glycerine, a bowl of soapy water.

Thread the string through the drinking straws and tie to make a loop. Add some glycerine to your bowl of soapy water and dip in your circle of string to make a film of soap. Pull upwards on your straw handles to fill the soapy film with air. Can you make it bounce up and down? Maybe you can make a giant bubble.

Three-dimensional bubble shapes

You will need: narrow plastic drinking straws, pipe-cleaners, PVA glue, a paintbrush, scissors, some thread, a bowl of soapy water.

1. Cut the straws into 8cm and 4cm long pieces.

2. Make a selection of 3D shapes (a cube, a triangular prism, a pyramid) joining the corners with small pieces (about 3cm) of pipe-cleaner. Fix the corners with a dab of PVA glue.

3. Attach a thread to one side of each of the shapes and dip them into the soapy solution. Interesting bubbles will form. Look at the bubble shapes closely and try to make a sketch of the shapes that have formed. Instead of bubbles with air contained inside them, here the air is on the outside.

Shaped bubble pictures.

AIR HAS WEIGHT

Weight is the force by which substances or objects are pulled towards the Earth by gravity.

If a substance such as air (which is a mixture of gases) exists, it must have a weight. Air is very light so it is very difficult to show that it has weight.

The apple pushes the air away as it falls.

Hold a number of different objects one by one. Which do you think is the heaviest? Which is the lightest?

Blow some soap bubbles. Catch a bubble in your hand. It is full of air. Do you think it is heavy?

Weighing air

You will need: a small tray of water, marbling inks, two balloons, a piece of dowel rod, thread, two bulldog clips.

2. Hang the dowel rod by a thread at its mid point, and attach the balloons using the bulldog clips at each end of the rod. You will need to move the clips carefully so that they balance and the rod is horizontal.

3. Ask a friend to hold the balance steady while you remove one balloon and blow it up. Tie the balloon at the neck and hang it back in its place. What happens when your friend lets go of the balance?

1. Put a few drops of marbling ink in the tray of water and swirl them around. Dip your balloons into the tray. The inks will make an interesting pattern on the surface of the balloons.

4. Look at the marbled pattern on the balloon. Did you notice how the pattern changed as you blew up the balloon and increased the volume of air inside it?

Lighter air

When air is heated it expands (gets bigger). The particles of warm air move further apart and take up more space. The air is lighter because it is less dense. This causes warm air to rise above colder, heavier air.

How warm does the air feel around a lighted candle? Feel the warm air rising above the flame, but don't put your hand any nearer the flame than 30cm.

Have you seen a hot-air balloon rise into the sky? Read about the Montgolfier brothers from France who designed the first hot-air balloon.

Warm air rises

You will need: thin card, a pair of compasses, a pencil, a ruler, scissors, felt-tip pens, paint and some thread.

1. Draw two circles, radius 8cm, on thin card. On one circle draw a spiral snake and decorate it with felt-tip pens. Divide the second circle into eighths and draw an inner circle 2cm from the centre. Cut from the edge to the inner circle as shown, and use a ruler to bend one side of the blades up and the other down.

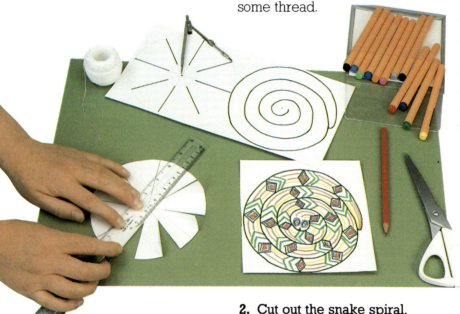

2. Cut out the snake spiral. Thread a piece of cotton through the circle's centre (the head of the snake) and hang it over a warm radiator. The warm air moving upwards will make your snake turn.

3. Paint the blades brightly and hang this circle also over a warm radiator. Watch what happens. Do you think it would make a difference if the green blades were bent up and the blue blades bent down?

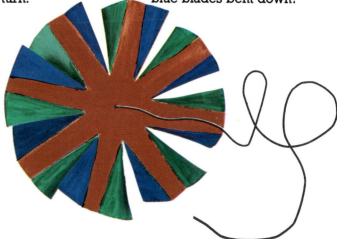

AIR PRESSURE

Blow out your cheeks so they are full of air. Press the sides of your cheeks. Can you feel the air pressing against your hands? You can feel air too in a blown-up balloon, or the tyres of a car or bicycle. As we blow more and more air into a balloon or a tyre, the air becomes compressed – the particles of air are squashed together. We say the air pressure is high – it is pressing to get out.

What happens if you inflate a balloon with too much air? Watch the weather forecast on the television. You will see areas of high pressure and areas of low pressure on the map. The air in the areas of high pressure pushes out into the areas of low pressure, and this causes windy weather. Have you travelled in a hovercraft? The pressure of air in the inflated skirt lifts the hovercraft off the ground and the sea.

A hovercraft

You will need: a margarine carton, scissors, and a balloon.

1. Make a hole in the centre of the margarine carton with your scissors, and push the neck of the balloon through the hole. Blow up the balloon, but do not tie it at the neck.

2. Put the carton on a table and give it a little push. The air in the inflated balloon forms a cushion of air inside the carton and then tries to escape from around the edges. The friction between the carton and the table is greatly reduced which allows it to glide along. This is why a hovercraft can travel across land or water so easily. Hovercrafts are also known as ACVs – air-cushion vehicles. Experiment with different shaped cartons or lids, and different sizes of balloons. Decorate your hovercraft with paints.

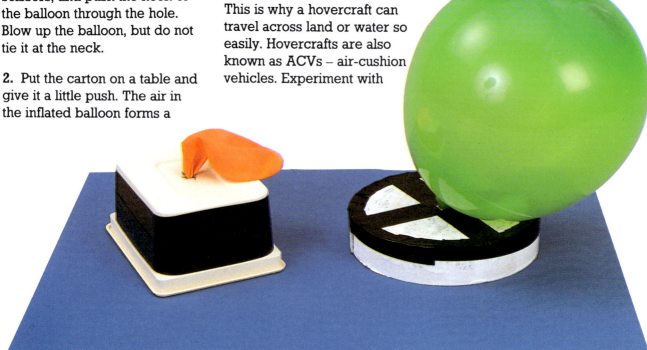

MOVING AIR

13

We can feel air if it is moving. A very light breeze will stir the leaves on the trees and make ripples on water.

Go outside on a calm day. Can you see any signs that tell you that the air is moving? You can make your own moving air. Blow through a straw and feel the air come out at the other end. On a hot day, people use fans to make a breeze to help them keep cool.

Blown ink trees

You will need: paints, small pieces of sponge, a paper tissue, Indian ink, a thin straw, and white paper.

1. Make a background with blue and green paint. Use a sponge to spread the paint across the paper. You can dab away some paint with a paper tissue to give the effect of clouds. Leave your background to dry.

2. Make an India ink blob as the base of your tree trunk. Use a thin straw to blow branches and roots.

A paper fan

You will need: a sheet of A3 paper, scissors, a ruler, a pencil, glue, a thin strip (2cm) of card, felt-tip pens.

1. Fold the sheet of paper in a zigzag. Use the strip of card to keep the widths even.

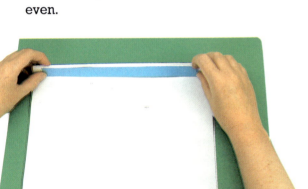

2. Cut the folded paper in half. Glue the two pieces together to make a long zigzag. Draw a pencil line 2cm from the bottom edge.

3. Cut some pieces from one side of the folded paper. Unfold and decorate with felt-tip pens. Glue the fan-folds together at the base below the line.

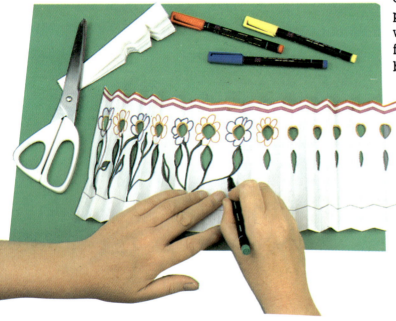

4. The finished fan. Wave your fan. Can you feel the air moving?

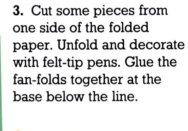

A paper waver

You will need: coloured tissue paper, cold water paste, scissors, a sheet of A4 sugar paper.

1. Cut some strips of coloured tissue paper and glue them along the bottom of the sheet of sugar paper.

2. Roll the sugar paper into a handle. (A plant support is useful to start the roll.) Glue the end and leave it to dry.

3. Take your waver outside to see if there is a breeze. Which way is the wind blowing? If it is a still day, run with your waver. Why do the streamers lift in the air?

A wind sock

You will need: A plastic bin liner, a black pen, scissors, strong glue, acrylic paints, thin wire, adhesive tape, and a plant support.

1. Draw a fish on the bin liner, with the fish's mouth at the joined end.

4. Decorate your fish with acrylic paint.

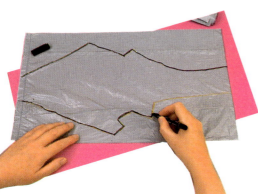

2. Cut out your fish leaving the mouth joined.

3. Open out the fish and put a line of glue around the edge. Close the two sides together, sticking them to one another, and leave to dry.

5. Make a loop with your piece of thin wire. Cut the mouth of the fish to fit over the loop. Attach the fish with glue and adhesive tape.

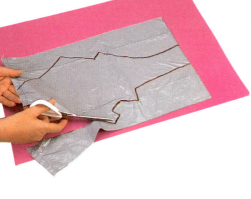

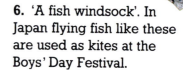

6. 'A fish windsock'. In Japan flying fish like these are used as kites at the Boys' Day Festival.

WIND STRENGTH

When air is moving we call it wind. Wind can be of different strengths and travel at different speeds. Light winds are sometimes called low winds, and strong winds are sometimes called high winds. Winds can range from light breezes to gales and hurricanes. Sir Francis Beaufort, an English admiral in the Navy, invented a scale to show the force of wind for sailors at sea.

Beaufort Number	Wind force (mph)
0 calm	less than 1
1 light air	1 – 3
2 light breeze	4 – 7
3 gentle breeze	8 – 12
4 moderate breeze	13 – 18
5 fresh breeze	19 – 24
6 strong breeze	25 – 31
7 near gale	32 – 38
8 gale	39 – 46
9 strong gale	47 – 54
10 storm	55 – 63
11 violent storm	64 – 72
12 hurricane	more than 72

Have you heard the shipping forecasts on the radio? Why do you think the wind measurements are important to people at sea? Look at some trees. How can you tell when there is a high wind? What might happen to an umbrella in a very high wind?

A desert landscape

You will need: a tray, paper, sand, a ruler, a pencil, paints, a hairdryer.

1. Wind plays a part in shaping the Earth. A high wind blows the sand on beaches and in deserts into dunes. Place a piece of paper on the bottom of your tray. Cover the paper with sand. Level the surface with a ruler.

2. Use a hairdryer to make a wind. Hold it still near one corner of the tray and let the air blow gently across the sand. As the sand is blown, you will begin to see the paper underneath. When this happens, stop the flow of air and draw the shape that is revealed on the paper. Turn the hairdryer on again and blow across the sand. As a larger area of paper is uncovered, draw another outline of the new shape. Continue to do this, and you will have a record of how the sand was moved by the air. Have dunes formed at the back of the tray? What happens if the direction of the wind changes? Try moving the position of the hairdryer to find out.

3. Paint the pattern of the lines you have drawn in different shades of the same colour.

4. 'Moving sands'. The source of the wind was at the bottom right of the picture. Can you imagine the dunes building up on the right?

An anemometer

An anemometer measures the speed of wind.
You will need: four yoghurt pots, balsa wood (0.5cm thick), paper, paints, brush, glue, a cork, a headed pin, a bead, a washing-up liquid bottle, sand, and a stop-clock.

1. Cover the yoghurt pots with paper. Paint three pots one colour and the fourth another (here it is red). Cut two strips of balsa wood (30cm long) and stick them together at right angles. Glue the pots to the ends facing clockwise.

2. Use the pin to fix the cups on to the cork in a sand-filled bottle.
Place a bead between the balsa wood strips and the cork, so the cups turn easily.

3. Stand your anemometer outside. Use a stopwatch and count how many turns the red cup makes per 10 seconds. Measure the wind speed on different days and keep a record of your findings.

WIND DIRECTION

The movement of air and direction of the wind are influenced by the air pressure and the air temperature.

High-pressure air flows into areas of low pressure. Warm air will rise causing colder currents of air to flow beneath.

A wind is known by the direction from which it blows. For example, a north wind blows from the north.

Watch smoke come out of a chimney, or study the clouds in the sky. They will give you clues to tell you which way the wind is blowing. What other clues can you find?
Notice the designs of different weather vanes. Why do you think they are placed high up on buildings?

Lines called isobars on a weather map join points of equal air pressure.

A WEATHER VANE

You will need: strong card, a craft knife, glue, a metal ruler, plastic drinking straws, paints, a washing-up liquid bottle, sand, two pieces of wood, a plant support, an elastic band, and a compass.

1. Use the craft knife to cut a vane from strong card. The tail of the pointer needs a large surface area. Use strong glue to fix a straw to the vane at an equal distance from both ends.

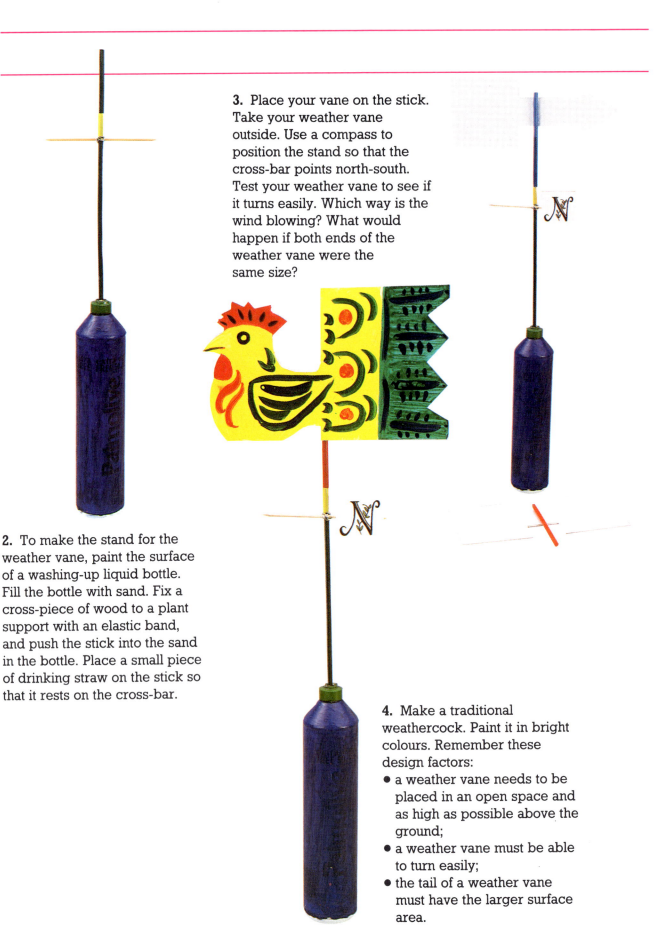

3. Place your vane on the stick. Take your weather vane outside. Use a compass to position the stand so that the cross-bar points north-south. Test your weather vane to see if it turns easily. Which way is the wind blowing? What would happen if both ends of the weather vane were the same size?

2. To make the stand for the weather vane, paint the surface of a washing-up liquid bottle. Fill the bottle with sand. Fix a cross-piece of wood to a plant support with an elastic band, and push the stick into the sand in the bottle. Place a small piece of drinking straw on the stick so that it rests on the cross-bar.

4. Make a traditional weathercock. Paint it in bright colours. Remember these design factors:
- a weather vane needs to be placed in an open space and as high as possible above the ground;
- a weather vane must be able to turn easily;
- the tail of a weather vane must have the larger surface area.

WIND CAN TURN

21

Wind can make things turn in a circular motion. We use this to harness the power of the wind. Windmills are positioned to face into the wind, where the wind is most powerful. The wind catches the sails of the windmill and makes them turn.

Windmills have been used since ancient times to grind corn, and later for pumping water. Nowadays windmills can be used to generate (make) electricity.

Find out about different windmill designs. How are fantails used on some windmills?

A paper windmill

You will need: coloured paper, scissors, plastic drinking straws, a pipe-cleaner, a pair of compasses, and double-sided adhesive tape.

1. Fold a square of paper along the diagonals. Cut half-way along each diagonal towards the centre. Fold over alternate points and fix at the centre with a small piece of adhesive tape.

2. Make a bend at the end of the pipe-cleaner. Pierce a hole in the centre of the windmill with the point of the compasses. Thread the pipe-cleaner through the windmill, a short piece of drinking straw, then through one end of a straw. This is the handle. Bend over the pipe-cleaner so that the windmill is held firm.

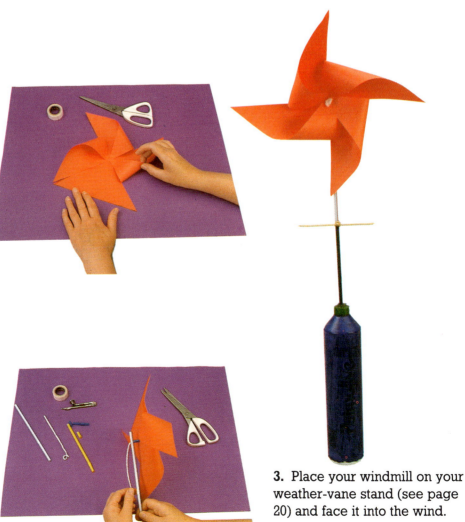

3. Place your windmill on your weather-vane stand (see page 20) and face it into the wind.

A double windmill

You will need: two sheets of different coloured paper, a small plate, scissors, plastic drinking straws, a pipe-cleaner, a pair of compasses, and double-sided adhesive tape.

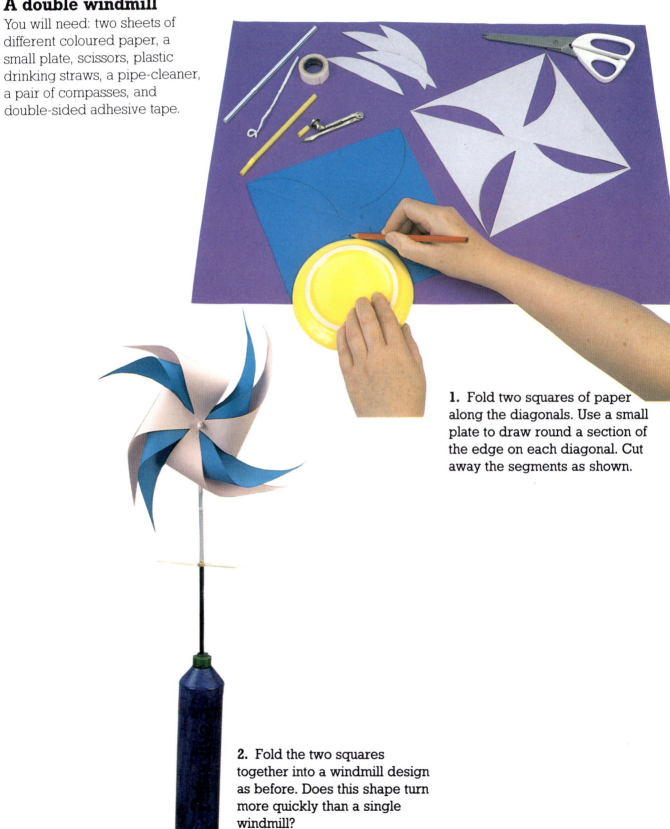

1. Fold two squares of paper along the diagonals. Use a small plate to draw round a section of the edge on each diagonal. Cut away the segments as shown.

2. Fold the two squares together into a windmill design as before. Does this shape turn more quickly than a single windmill?

Wind sails

You will need: balsa wood (0.5cm and 1cm thick), a craft knife, a metal ruler, paper, glue, a headed pin, two small beads, and felt-tip pens.

1. Use the craft knife and metal ruler to cut a strip of balsa wood from a thin sheet of wood. Cut a handle, about 12cm long, from a 1cm-thick sheet of wood.

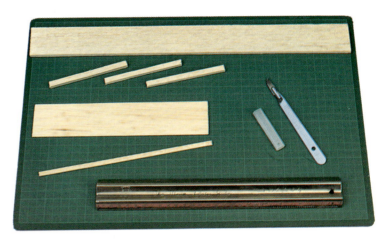

2. Glue a piece of paper (7cm×6cm) to one end of the thin strip of balsa wood. Turn the strip over and glue a second piece of paper (the same size) on the other end, facing in the other direction. Use the pin to attach the sail to the handle. Thread a bead on either side of the sail to act as pivots.

3. Coloured sails are attractive. Hold your sail in front of you. Walk quickly and see what happens. Try running with your wind sail. Pin your sail so that the blades face in the other direction. Does this affect the result?

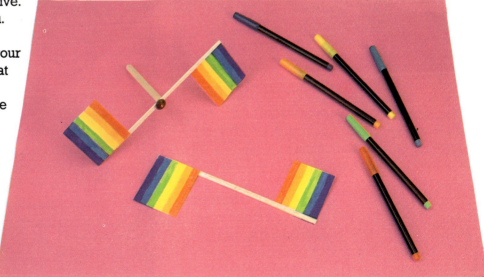

24

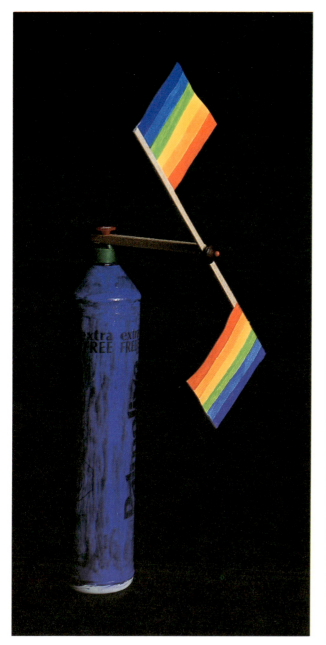

4. Fix the wind sail to a stand (see page 20).

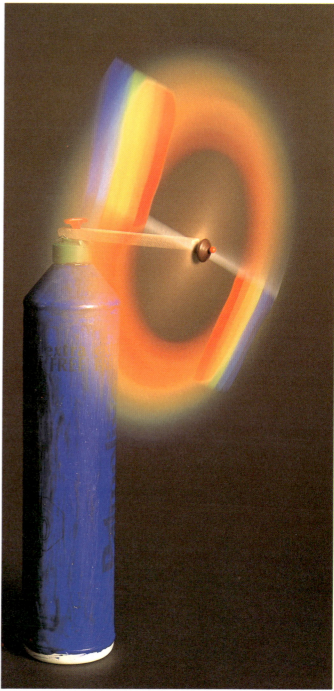

5. 'Sails in the wind'. Air presses against the blades and pushes them out of the way. The next sail comes into position and the same thing happens. The sails turn round and round. Try two sails fixed together at right angles. Do these turn faster? How many sails are there on a real windmill?

WIND CAN PUSH

Sailing boats are powered by the wind. Early sail boats had square sails. They were blown along by the wind – they ran with the wind. Later, triangular sails were introduced. By changing the position of the sails, a boat can sail into the wind as well as being pushed from behind. Moving the sails can also make the boat change direction. Large sailing ships, such as clippers, had many sails.

Nowadays sails are used on yachts and wind-surfing boards on water and on land. Watch how the sailors and surfers control their sails to catch the wind.

A land-racer

You will need: paper, thin card, thin sticks (such as wooden meat skewers), PVA glue, a pencil, a craft knife, a metal ruler, four plastic bottle-tops, beads or plastic drinking straws, a metal knitting needle, a night-light candle.

1. Draw a plan of a box shape, for the body of your vehicle. Fold your pattern to see where you need tabs to join your model. Transfer the design to the card. Score (do not cut) along the lines so that your card folds easily.

2. Glue the body together. Warm the tip of the knitting needle in the night-light. Melt a small hole in the centre of the four bottle-tops. These are the wheels. Rest the hot needle on a block of wood.

WARNING: DO NOT TOUCH THE TIP OF THE NEEDLE. IT WILL BE VERY HOT.

3. Use the thin sticks as axles. Place a small piece of drinking straw, or a bead, between each wheel and the body. Cut some different shaped sails from thin card.

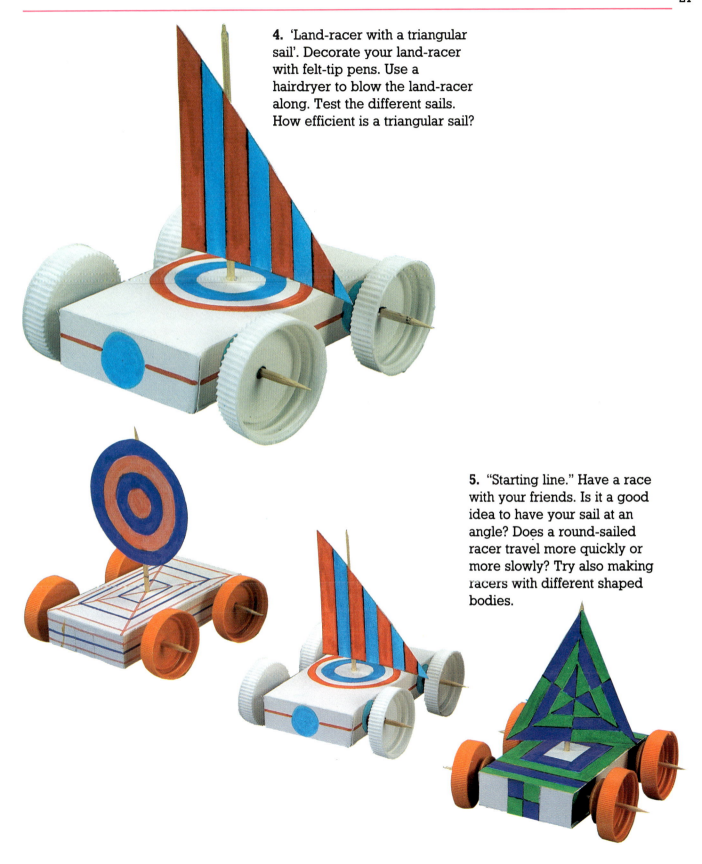

4. 'Land-racer with a triangular sail'. Decorate your land-racer with felt-tip pens. Use a hairdryer to blow the land-racer along. Test the different sails. How efficient is a triangular sail?

5. "Starting line." Have a race with your friends. Is it a good idea to have your sail at an angle? Does a round-sailed racer travel more quickly or more slowly? Try also making racers with different shaped bodies.

AIR SUPPORTS

Any object will float in air if it is lighter than the volume of air it is displacing. If there was no air, objects would fall straight to the ground. Heavy objects push the air away as they fall. Light objects float on the air – the air supports them.

The hot air in a hot-air balloon is lighter than the surrounding air, so people can fly. Why do helium balloons float and air-filled balloons sink? Have you watched seeds floating in the air? They are quite light so they float before falling to the ground. Air pushes against the surface of sycamore seed 'wings'. They spin like the wind-sails on page 23.

A feather floats.

A ball falls.

A paper helicopter

You will need: a sheet of A4 paper, a pencil, scissors, felt-tip pens, and a paper clip.

1. Fold the paper into eight rectangles. Use one rectangle and divide this into quarters. Draw two lines from the centre side to the centre base. Cut to a point. Cut from the top centre as shown.

2. Fold one wing forward and the other back. Colour the top surface of the wings with felt-tip pens. Try out different patterns. Fix the paper clip to the point.

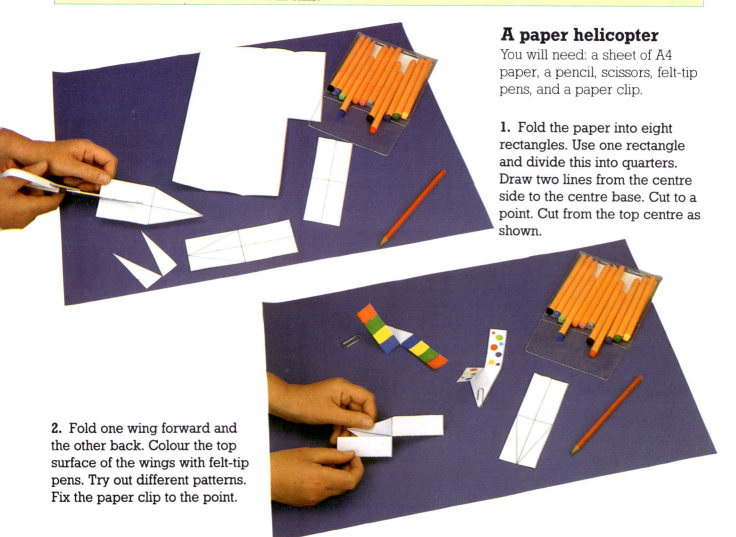

3. Stand on a chair and drop your helicopter. Watch what happens. Why do you think the paper clip is important?

FURTHER IDEAS

Tissue-paper mobile

Spinning blades

1. Fix your blades (see page 11) vertically on a stand.

2. Watch them turn in the wind.

1. Make some shapes from wire. Place the shapes on tissue paper and surround the edge of the wire with glue. Fold the tissue paper over the top of the wire. Leave to dry.

2. Trim the tissue at the edge of the shape. Decorate with sequins and pieces of different coloured tissue paper.

An illustrated dictionary

Make an illustrated dictionary of words which have links with air and wind.

Here are some examples:
airborne	wind break
air brush	wind cheater
air lock	wind instrument

You could cover your book with a colourful bubble pattern design (see page 8). For this, use Indian ink instead of paint so that the colours are fast.

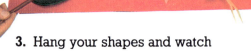

3. Hang your shapes and watch them move in a draught of air.

GLOSSARY

Air
The atmosphere surrounding the Earth. An invisible mixture of gases, mainly nitrogen and oxygen.

Air current
A moving stream of air.

Air pressure
The effect of the weight of air pressing on an object, or substance.

Anemometer
An instrument for measuring wind speed.

Atmosphere
The envelope of gases which surrounds all the stars and planets.

Beaufort Scale
A series of numbers used by meteorologists and sailors to describe the force of wind.

Bubble
A spherical envelope of liquid containing air.

Compressed air
Air squeezed into a smaller volume. The air particles become squashed together making the air more dense.

Density
The weight of a substance per unit of volume.

Draught
A small current of air.

Gas
A substance which has no shape. It can fill all the space inside any container.

Hovercraft
An amphibious vehicle which travels on a cushion of air. They are also known as ACVs – air-cushion vehicles.

Oxygen
A colourless, odourless, tasteless gas essential to life. Oxygen is made by the plants of the Earth.

Particle
A tiny piece of something, for example, a particle of air.

Sail
A device designed to catch the wind, for example, a sail on a boat or a windmill.

Weather vane
An instrument for showing the direction of the wind.

Wind
Moving air.

Wind direction
A wind is known by the direction from which it blows. For example, a north wind blows from the north.

Wind power
The force of the wind which causes movement. It can be a turning force or a pushing force.

INDEX

ACVs 12, 31
air pressure 12, 31
air temperature 19
anemometer 18, 31
atmosphere 5, 31

balloon 12
Beaufort scale 17, 31
Boys' Day Festival 16
bubble art 7-9
bubble dome 8

clippers 25

density 10, 31
desert landscape 17-18
double windmill 22

Earth 5, 10
electricity 21

fantails 21
floating 28-29
force 10

gases 6, 31
gravity 10

helium balloons 28
high pressure 19
high winds 17
hot-air balloon 28
hovercraft 12, 31

land-racer 25-27
low pressure 19
low winds 17

mobile 30
moving air 13

nitrogen 5

oxygen 5, 31

paper fan 14
paper helicopter 28
paper waver 15
pollution 6

sailing boats 25
sails 23, 25, 31
scientist 5
seeds 28
shipping 17
spinning blades 30

tyres 12

warm air 11, 19
weather vanes 19-20, 31
weighing air 10
weight 10
wind direction 19, 31
wind power 21-24, 31
wind sock 16
wind strength 17-18
windmills 21-24